Taste of Ch

Hot Cocoa
AND OTHER WINTRY BEVERAGES
• COOKBOOK •
& Inspiration for the Season

Print ISBN 978-1-61626-852-7

eBook Editions:
Adobe Digital Edition (.epub) 978-1-62029-090-3
Kindle and MobiPocket Edition (.prc) 978-1-62029-091-0

All scripture quotations are taken from the King James Version of the Bible.

Published by Barbour Publishing, Inc., P.O. Box 719, Uhrichsville, Ohio 44683, www.barbourbooks.com

Our mission is to publish and distribute inspirational products offering exceptional value and biblical encouragement to the masses.

ecpa Member of the
Evangelical Christian
Publishers Association

Printed in the United States of America.

Taste of Christmas

Hot Cocoa
AND OTHER WINTRY BEVERAGES
• COOKBOOK •
& Inspiration for the Season

BARBOUR
PUBLISHING

Contents

It's beginning to taste a lot like Christmas! . . .with these delicious holiday drink recipes including everything from traditional hot cocoa to teas, coffees, lattes, and more, all perfect for warming up your heart—and the hearts of the ones you love— this Christmas.

Hot Cocoa Delights

Fear not: for, behold, I bring you good tidings of great joy, which shall be to all people. For unto you is born this day in the city of David a Saviour, which is Christ the Lord.

LUKE 2:10–11

Snowy Cinnamon Cocoa

4 cups milk
1 cup chocolate syrup
1 teaspoon ground cinnamon

Whipped topping
¼ cup semisweet chocolate chips

Place milk and chocolate syrup in microwave-safe bowl and stir. Cook on high for 3 to 4 minutes or until hot. Stir in cinnamon. Pour into 4 large mugs and garnish with whipped topping and chocolate chips.

World's Best Cocoa

¼ cup cocoa powder   ⅛ teaspoon salt
½ cup sugar   4 cups milk
⅓ cup hot water   ¾ teaspoon vanilla

Mix cocoa, sugar, water, and salt in saucepan. Stir constantly over medium
heat until mixture boils. Continue to stir and boil for 1 minute.
Add milk and heat (do not boil). Remove from heat and add vanilla;
stir well. Pour into 4 mugs and serve immediately.

Christmassy Hot Chocolate Float

2 packets instant
  hot chocolate mix
2 cups hot water

2 scoops vanilla ice cream
Holiday sprinkles

Prepare hot chocolate according to packet directions. Add 1 scoop of ice cream to each prepared mug of hot chocolate. Serve topped with holiday sprinkles.

Creamy Dreamy Hot Chocolate

1 (14 ounce) can sweetened
   condensed milk
½ cup cocoa powder

2 teaspoons vanilla
⅛ teaspoon salt
6½ cups hot water

Combine condensed milk, cocoa powder, vanilla, and salt in large
saucepan; mix well. Over medium heat, slowly stir in water.
Cook until heated through, stirring frequently.

Hot Chocolate Eggnog

4 cups eggnog
½ cup chocolate syrup
¼ teaspoon ground nutmeg

2½ teaspoons vanilla
Whipped topping
Additional ground nutmeg

In large saucepan, combine eggnog, chocolate syrup, and nutmeg.
Heat through over low heat approximately 10 minutes (do not boil).
Remove from heat and stir in vanilla. Pour into mugs and
top with whipped topping and nutmeg.

Honeyed Hot Chocolate

4 cups hot milk   4 tablespoons honey
4 tablespoons cocoa powder

Warm milk in medium saucepan over medium-low heat
(do not boil). Add cocoa powder and honey. Stir until
cocoa powder is dissolved. Serve immediately.

Raspberry Cocoa Mix

3 cups instant hot chocolate mix   1 (.13 ounce) packet unsweetened
                                       raspberry drink mix

Blend ingredients well. Store in airtight container.
To prepare: Add 2 heaping tablespoons to 1 cup hot water.

Double Marshmallow Hot Cocoa

4 cups milk
1¼ cup marshmallow cream
⅓ cup sugar
¼ cup cocoa powder

⅛ teaspoon salt
½ teaspoon vanilla
Miniature marshmallows

Add milk, marshmallow cream, sugar, cocoa powder, salt, and vanilla to large saucepan. Cook over medium-high heat, stirring constantly until sugar dissolves and mixture begins to bubble. Set heat to low and cook until most of the marshmallow cream dissolves, but leave small chunks in the hot chocolate. Serve in mugs and top with miniature marshmallows.

Chocolate Mint Cocoa

10 chocolate sandwich cookies,
   coarsely chopped
3 cups milk

½ cup chocolate syrup
½ teaspoon peppermint extract

Place all ingredients in blender; cover and blend on high speed until
well blended. Pour into 2-quart saucepan. Cook on medium-high
heat until heated through, stirring frequently. Serve hot.

White Chocolate Hot Cocoa

3 cups half-and-half, divided
¾ cup white chocolate chips
3 cinnamon sticks
⅛ teaspoon ground nutmeg

1 teaspoon vanilla
¼ teaspoon almond extract
Ground cinnamon

In medium saucepan, combine ¼ cup half-and-half, white chocolate chips, cinnamon sticks, and nutmeg. Whisk over low heat until chocolate is melted. Remove cinnamon sticks. Add remaining half-and-half. Whisk until heated through. Remove from heat. Stir in vanilla and almond extracts. Pour into cups or mugs. Sprinkle with cinnamon if desired.

Steaming Mocha Cocoa

2 cups milk
1 tablespoon cocoa powder
2 tablespoons brown sugar

1 tablespoon ground coffee
1 teaspoon vanilla

Heat all ingredients in small saucepan and whisk until steaming.
Strain and pour into 2 mugs.

Peanut Butter Hot Chocolate

1 packet instant hot chocolate mix   2 tablespoons creamy peanut butter

Prepare hot chocolate according to directions on packet.
Stir in peanut butter. Serve immediately.

Hot Chocolate Truffle

4 cups milk
6 ounces dark baking chocolate,
    chopped
3 tablespoons brown sugar

¾ teaspoon instant espresso powder
1 teaspoon vanilla
Peppermint whipped topping

In large saucepan, heat milk over medium heat until bubbles form around sides of pan (do not boil). Remove from heat. Mix in chocolate, brown sugar, espresso powder, and vanilla until smooth. Return to heat; cook and stir until heated through. Pour into mugs and serve with Peppermint whipped topping (recipe follows).

Peppermint Whipped Topping

½ cup heavy whipping cream
1 tablespoon sugar
⅛ teaspoon peppermint extract

1 tablespoon crushed red-and-
white peppermint candies

In small bowl, beat whipping cream until it begins to thicken. Add sugar and peppermint extract; beat until stiff peaks form. Garnish with peppermint candies. Use this to top off your favorite Christmas beverages.

Peanut Butter Chocolate Cocoa

½ cup chocolate syrup
½ cup creamy peanut butter
Ground cinnamon

4 cups milk
Miniature marshmallows

Stir chocolate syrup, peanut butter, cinnamon, and milk in
saucepan over medium-low heat until smooth. Remove from heat.
Serve in mugs topped with miniature marshmallows.

Coconut Hot Chocolate

2 tablespoons cocoa powder
⅓ cup boiling water
1 (15 ounce) can coconut milk
¼ cup packed brown sugar

Pinch salt
¼ cup bittersweet chocolate,
  chopped
1 teaspoon vanilla

Whisk cocoa powder into ⅓ cup boiling water. In separate saucepan, combine coconut milk, brown sugar, and salt. Simmer, stirring constantly, until sugar is dissolved. Whisk in hot cocoa and chocolate pieces until smooth. Stir in vanilla. Serve immediately.

Hot Fudge Sundae Cocoa

1¾ cups half-and-half
1 cup milk
¾ cup hot fudge ice-cream topping
⅛ teaspoon ground cinnamon
2 cups vanilla ice cream, divided

Whipped topping
Hot fudge ice-cream topping, warmed
Maraschino cherries

Combine half-and-half, milk, hot fudge topping, and cinnamon in 2-quart saucepan. Cook over medium heat, stirring constantly until mixture just comes to a boil. Remove from heat. Pour 1-cup servings of cocoa into 4 large mugs, adding ½ cup ice cream for each serving. Serve with whipped topping, warm hot fudge, and a cherry.

Peppermint Twist White Hot Chocolate

4 cups milk
3 ounces white chocolate, chopped
⅓ cup candy canes or peppermint candies, crushed

⅛ teaspoon salt
Whipped topping
Additional candy canes, crushed

Bring milk to a simmer in saucepan. Reduce heat to medium-low. Add white chocolate, crushed candy canes, and salt; whisk until smooth. Ladle into mugs, dividing equally. Serve with whipped topping and additional crushed candy canes.

Rich Parisian Chocolate

1 cup whole milk
¾ cup heavy cream
¼ cup sugar

5 ounces semisweet chocolate,
  chopped
Whipped topping

In saucepan, over medium-high heat, bring milk, cream, and sugar to a simmer (heating just until bubbly around the edges of the liquid). Remove from heat and add chocolate, stirring until mixture is smooth. If necessary, return pan to low heat while stirring with a wooden spoon until chocolate is melted. Serve in small mugs with whipped topping.

Thin Mint Cocoa

½ cup sugar
¼ cup instant hot chocolate mix
⅓ cup hot water

4 cups whole milk
1 teaspoon vanilla
1 teaspoon peppermint extract

Mix sugar and hot chocolate mix in hot water until completely
dissolved. Bring mixture to a boil; stir for 2 minutes.
Add milk, vanilla, and peppermint extracts to mixture.
Continue cooking until hot, but do not boil. Serve hot.

Twist of Orange Hot Chocolate

2 cups milk
1 (1x2 inch) orange peel strip
(orange part only)
⅛ teaspoon ground cinnamon

½ teaspoon instant espresso powder
4 ounces semisweet chocolate,
grated

Combine all ingredients in saucepan. Stir over low heat until chocolate melts. Increase heat and bring to a boil, stirring often. Immediately remove from heat and whisk until frothy. Return to heat and bring to a boil again. Repeat heating and whisking once again. Discard orange peel. Pour into mugs and serve.

Italian Hot Cocoa

½ cup cocoa powder   1 cup milk
⅓ cup sugar   ⅛ teaspoon vanilla
1 teaspoon cornstarch   Ground cinnamon
1 cup water, divided   Miniature marshmallows

In medium saucepan, stir together cocoa, sugar, and cornstarch. Stir in ½ cup water and place on stovetop over low heat. Stir in remaining water, milk, and vanilla. Cook over medium-low heat, stirring frequently until mixture is thick enough to coat a spoon, approximately 10 to 12 minutes. Serve in mugs and top with ground cinnamon and miniature marshmallows.

Candy Cane Cocoa

4 cups milk
3 (1 ounce) squares semisweet
    chocolate, chopped

4 peppermint candy canes, crushed
1 cup whipped topping
4 small peppermint candy canes

In medium saucepan, heat milk until hot but not boiling.

Whisk in chocolate and crushed candy canes until smooth.

Pour hot cocoa into 4 mugs. Garnish with whipped topping.

Serve each with a miniature candy cane stirring stick.

Spiced Hot Cocoa

6 cups milk
3 tablespoons cocoa powder
3 tablespoons sugar
1 teaspoon vanilla

1 teaspoon ground cinnamon
¼ teaspoon chili powder
¼ teaspoon ground nutmeg
¼ teaspoon ground cloves

Heat milk in saucepan over medium-low heat until warm; stir cocoa powder and sugar into milk until dissolved. Add vanilla, cinnamon, chili powder, nutmeg, and cloves. Heat an additional 3 to 5 minutes, stirring occasionally. Serve immediately.

Festive Hot Cocoa

1 packet instant hot chocolate mix   Red and green candy sprinkles
Whipped topping   1 cherry

Prepare instant hot chocolate as directed on packet. Spoon on whipped topping. Top with candy sprinkles and a cherry before serving.

Maple Hot Cocoa with Marshmallows

¼ cup sugar
1 tablespoon cocoa powder
⅛ teaspoon salt
¼ cup hot water
¾ tablespoon butter

4 cups milk
1 teaspoon maple flavoring
1 teaspoon vanilla
14 large marshmallows

In large saucepan, combine sugar, cocoa, and salt. Stir in hot water and butter; bring to boil. Add milk, maple flavoring, vanilla, and 10 marshmallows. Heat through, stirring frequently until marshmallows are completely melted. Serve in mugs and top with marshmallows.

Cinnamon Cocoa Mix

1¾ cups nonfat dry milk powder
1 cup powdered sugar
½ cup powdered nondairy creamer

½ cup cocoa powder
½ teaspoon ground cinnamon
1¼ cup miniature marshmallows

In bowl, combine milk powder, powdered sugar, creamer, cocoa, cinnamon, and marshmallows. Mix well. Store in airtight container for up to 3 months. To prepare: Dissolve about 4 tablespoons cinnamon cocoa mix in 1 cup hot milk.

Caramel Hot Cocoa

4 cups nonfat dry milk powder
¾ cup cocoa powder
½ cup sugar
8 cups water

1 caramel-filled chocolate bar,
    chopped
Whipped topping

In slow cooker, combine milk powder, cocoa, and sugar. Gradually
add water and stir until smooth. Cover and cook on low for 3 to
4 hours or until hot. Add chocolate bar and stir until melted.
Garnish with whipped topping.

Winter Warmer Cocoa Drink

2 packets instant hot chocolate mix
3 cups freshly brewed coffee
¼ cup half-and-half

½ teaspoon rum extract
¼ cup whipped topping
Ground cinnamon

In small saucepan, whisk together hot chocolate mix, coffee,
half-and-half, and rum extract until heated through. Pour into mugs.
Garnish with whipped topping and sprinkle with cinnamon before serving.

Minty Hot Chocolate

2 cups chocolate malted
 milk powder, divided
1 cup butter mints

3 cups nonfat dry milk powder
1½ cups instant chocolate
 drink mix

In food processor, combine 1 cup malted milk powder and mints; cover
and process until smooth. Pour into large bowl. Add milk powder,
chocolate drink mix, and remaining malted milk powder; stir well.
Store in airtight container. To prepare: Combine ¼ cup drink mix
and ¾ cup hot water; stir until dissolved.

Triple Chocolate Mint Cocoa Mix

6 cups nonfat milk powder
1 (16 ounce) package powdered
  sugar
2 (8 ounce) jars chocolate-flavored
  powdered nondairy creamer

1 (7.5 ounce) package round
  peppermint candies, finely ground
¼ cup cocoa powder
1 teaspoon salt

Combine all ingredients in large bowl. To serve, pour 6 ounces
boiling water over 3 tablespoons cocoa mix. Stir until well blended.
Store mix in airtight container in refrigerator.

Brown Sugar Hot Cocoa

3 ounces unsweetened chocolate
⅓ cup water
4 cups hot milk

¾ cup packed brown sugar
2 pinches salt

In double boiler, melt chocolate in water. Slowly stir in milk, brown sugar, and salt. Whisk until chocolate is smooth and blended. Serve immediately.

Sweet and Spicy Hot Chocolate

½ cup semisweet chocolate chips
½ cup whole milk
1 teaspoon instant coffee granules

⅓ teaspoon ground cinnamon
⅛ teaspoon hot chili powder
½ cup cold whole milk

Combine chocolate chips and milk in microwave-safe bowl; cook on high, stirring every 30 seconds, until smooth. Stir in coffee, cinnamon, and hot chili powder until coffee granules are dissolved. Add cold milk and stir well. Strain into mugs and serve immediately.

Christmas Party Cocoa (for a Crowd)

4 cups sugar
3¼ cups cocoa powder
½ teaspoon salt
4 cups warm water
8 cups boiling water
4 gallons hot whole milk

Optional toppings:
Marshmallows
Whipped topping
Miniature chocolate chips
Miniature candy canes
Holiday sprinkles

In extra-large kettle, combine sugar, cocoa powder, salt, and warm water; mix well. Add additional boiling water; boil mixture for 10 minutes. Remove from heat and stir in hot milk. Serve in mugs with a variety of optional toppings so your holiday guests can top off their hot cocoa just the way they like it.

Snowy Cocoa

6 cups whipping cream
6 cups whole milk
1 teaspoon vanilla
1 (12 ounce) package white
   chocolate chips

Whipped topping
Miniature chocolate chips
6 candy canes, crushed

Stir together whipping cream, milk, vanilla, and white chocolate chips in slow cooker. Cover and cook on low for 2 hours, stirring occasionally until mixture is hot and white chocolate chips are melted. Stir well before serving. Pour into mugs and top with whipped topping, miniature chocolate chips, and crushed candy canes.

Christmassy
Coffee
Drinks

Glory to God in the highest, and on earth peace,
good will toward men.

Luke 2:14

Christmas Morning Coffee

1 pot (10 cups) brewed coffee
⅓ cup water
½ cup sugar
¼ cup cocoa powder

¼ teaspoon ground cinnamon
1 pinch grated nutmeg
Whipped topping (optional)

Prepare coffee. While coffee is brewing, heat water to low boil
in large saucepan. Stir in sugar, cocoa, cinnamon, and nutmeg.
Bring back to low boil for 1 minute, stirring occasionally.
Combine coffee with cocoa/spice mixture in saucepan. To serve,
pour into mugs and top with whipped topping if desired.

Cozy Christmas Coffee Mix

½ cup powdered nondairy creamer
¼ cup powdered sugar
2 tablespoons vanilla powder

2 cups nonfat dry milk powder
⅔ cup instant coffee granules
1⅛ cups miniature chocolate chips

Combine nondairy creamer, powdered sugar, vanilla powder, and milk
powder. Layer with coffee granules and chocolate chips. Mix all
ingredients to combine. To prepare: Add 3 to 4 teaspoons
of coffee mix to 1 cup boiling water.

Eggnog Coffee

1⅓ cups prepared eggnog   Whipped topping
2⅓ cups freshly brewed coffee   Ground nutmeg
  (dark roast)

Place eggnog in large saucepan. Cook and stir until heated through
(do not boil). Add freshly brewed coffee. Pour into mugs and
serve immediately with whipped topping and ground nutmeg.

Creamy Peppermint Coffee

6 ounces freshly brewed coffee   Miniature candy cane
1 scoop peppermint ice cream

Pour coffee into large mug and add scoop of ice cream.
Stir until slightly melted. Garnish with miniature candy cane stirrer.

Festive Eggnog Coffee

1¼ cups coffee-flavored ice cream
1½ cups prepared eggnog
1 cup freshly brewed dark roast
    coffee

Whipped topping
Ground nutmeg

Scoop ice cream into saucepan over low heat. Add eggnog and coffee and stir well. Heat until warmed through. Pour into 4 mugs and serve topped with whipped topping and ground nutmeg.

Spicy Coconut Coffee

2 tablespoons ground coffee
⅓ teaspoon crushed red pepper
2 whole cloves
1 (3 inch) cinnamon stick

2 cups water
½ cup coconut milk
1½ tablespoons honey

Combine ground coffee, crushed red pepper, cloves, and cinnamon stick in coffee filter of a drip coffee brewer. Pour water into water reservoir and set coffee to brew. Meanwhile, gently warm coconut milk in small saucepan over low heat. Add honey and stir until dissolved. Add freshly brewed coffee to coconut milk mixture and serve in mugs.

White Chocolate Coffee

3 ounces white chocolate, grated
2 cups whole milk

2 cups brewed coffee
Whipped topping (optional)

Place grated white chocolate and milk in microwave-safe bowl and heat for 2 minutes. Stir until mixture is smooth and chocolate is melted completely. Stir in coffee. Serve in large mugs and top with whipped topping if desired.

Pumpkin Spice Coffee

¼ cup ground coffee
1 teaspoon ground allspice
¾ teaspoon ground cinnamon

4 cups water
2 teaspoons half-and-half
1 teaspoon sugar

Mix coffee, allspice, and cinnamon in small bowl; place in coffee filter in coffeemaker. Pour water into coffeemaker then brew. When coffee has finished dripping, pour into 2 mugs. Stir in half-and-half and sugar. Serve.

Mocha Spiced Coffee

1½ teaspoons ground cinnamon
½ teaspoon ground nutmeg
5 cups freshly brewed coffee
1 cup milk

¼ cup packed brown sugar
⅓ cup chocolate syrup
1 teaspoon vanilla

Mix cinnamon and nutmeg with coffee grounds to make 5 cups
of coffee. Make coffee in coffeemaker. In heavy saucepan,
combine milk, brown sugar, and chocolate syrup. Cook over
low heat, stirring frequently and making sure milk does not boil.
Once sugar is dissolved, add vanilla and brewed coffee. Serve.

Cozy Fireside Coffee

2 cups powdered nondairy creamer 1 teaspoon ground cinnamon
1½ cups instant hot chocolate mix ⅓ teaspoon ground nutmeg
1½ cups instant coffee granules

Mix together powdered creamer, hot chocolate mix, instant coffee
granules, cinnamon, and nutmeg. Store in airtight container.
To prepare: Stir 3 teaspoons of mixture into 1 cup of hot water.

Spiced Coffee

8 cups freshly brewed coffee
¼ cup sugar
¼ cup chocolate syrup

½ teaspoon anise extract
3 cinnamon sticks
1½ teaspoons whole cloves

Combine coffee, sugar, chocolate syrup, and anise extract in 4-quart
slow cooker. Place cinnamon sticks and cloves in double thickness of
cheesecloth, bringing up corners of cloth and tying with string to form
a bag. Add to slow cooker. Cover and cook on low for 3 hours.
Discard spice bag before serving.

Creamy Spiced Coffee

¼ cup evaporated milk
2½ teaspoons powdered sugar
⅓ teaspoon ground cinnamon

⅛ teaspoon vanilla
1 cup freshly brewed strong coffee
Ground nutmeg

Pour milk into small mixing bowl; place mixer beaters in bowl.
Cover and freeze for approximately 30 minutes—just until ice crystals
begin to form. Add sugar, cinnamon, and vanilla; beat until thick and
fluffy. Pour ½ cup of mixture into each mug. Add freshly brewed coffee.
Sprinkle with nutmeg and serve immediately.

Maple Cream Coffee

¾ cup half-and-half   1¼ cups freshly brewed coffee
¼ cup maple syrup   Whipped topping

In small saucepan, combine half-and-half and maple syrup; cook and stir
over medium-low heat until heated through (do not boil). Divide evenly
between 2 cups. Top off with coffee and serve with whipped topping.

Chocolate Hazelnut Coffee

¾ cup hot water
¼ cup hot milk
2 teaspoons hazelnut-flavored
   instant coffee granules

1 teaspoon cocoa
1 tablespoon dark brown sugar
1 tablespoon whipped topping

Stir together first five ingredients. Pour into mugs. Top with whipped topping and serve immediately.

Toffee Coffee

½ cup heavy whipping cream
1 tablespoon powdered sugar
½ cup milk chocolate toffee bits

5 cups hot brewed coffee
Whipped topping
Butterscotch ice-cream topping

In small bowl, beat cream until it begins to thicken. Add powdered sugar; beat until stiff peaks form. Stir toffee bits into coffee; let stand for 1 minute. Strain and discard any undissolved toffee bits. Pour into mugs. Serve with whipped topping, drizzled with butterscotch syrup.

Creamy Marshmallow Coffee

6 ounces freshly brewed coffee   Ground cinnamon
¼ cup marshmallow cream

Pour coffee into large mug. Stir in marshmallow cream until lightly blended. Serve topped with ground cinnamon.

Coffee Mocha

1 cup freshly brewed coffee   1 tablespoon sugar
1 tablespoon cocoa powder   2 tablespoons milk

Pour coffee into mug. Stir in cocoa powder, sugar, and milk.

Butterscotch Coffee

8 cups hot brewed coffee
½ cup butterscotch chips
½ cup half-and-half

6 tablespoons sugar
Whipped topping

In large pitcher, stir coffee and butterscotch chips until chips
are melted. Stir in half-and-half and sugar. Pour into mugs.
Serve with whipped topping.

Mexican Coffee

½ cup packed brown sugar
6 cups warm water
½ cup ground coffee
½ ounce unsweetened chocolate

2 tablespoons ground cinnamon
1 tablespoon chamomile tea
2 whole cloves
½ teaspoon vanilla

In 3-quart saucepan, heat brown sugar until melted. Stir constantly to avoid scorching. Remove from heat and slowly stir in water. Add coffee, chocolate, cinnamon, tea, and cloves. Stir to mix thoroughly. Heat to boiling. Reduce heat and simmer for 15 minutes. Stir in vanilla. Strain coffee through 2 pieces of cheesecloth before serving.

Hot Buttered Coffee

¼ cup butter, softened
1 cup packed brown sugar
¾ teaspoon vanilla
½ teaspoon ground cinnamon

¼ teaspoon ground nutmeg
¼ teaspoon ground allspice
⅛ teaspoon ground cloves
Whipped topping

In small bowl, combine butter and brown sugar until crumbly. Beat in
vanilla and spices. (Cover and refrigerate leftover butter mixture for
up to 2 weeks.) For each serving, stir 1 tablespoon butter mixture
into 1 cup coffee. Garnish with whipped topping if desired.

Cinnamon Mocha Coffee

⅓ cup ground coffee (not instant)   2 tablespoons cocoa powder
¾ teaspoon ground cinnamon   1 teaspoon vanilla
1 cup milk   Cinnamon sticks
3 tablespoons sugar   Whipped topping

Combine coffee and ground cinnamon and place in coffee filter in
coffeemaker. Prepare 4 cups freshly brewed coffee. Meanwhile,
combine milk, sugar, cocoa, and vanilla in saucepan. Cook over
medium-low heat for 5 minutes or until small bubbles appear on sides
of pan (do not boil). Pour hot milk mixture into 4
mugs; add cinnamon-flavored coffee. Garnish with
cinnamon sticks and whipped topping.

Almond Macaroon Coffee

½ cup ground coffee
⅓ cup sugar

6 cups cold water
½ teaspoon almond extract

Place coffee granules in filter of drip coffeemaker. Add sugar to the empty coffeepot. Brew prepared coffee with cold water. When brewing cycle is done, stir in almond extract. Serve in mugs.

Gingerbread Coffee

½ cup molasses
¼ cup packed brown sugar
½ teaspoon baking soda
1 teaspoon ground ginger
¾ teaspoon ground cinnamon

6 cups freshly brewed coffee
1 cup half-and-half
1½ cups whipped topping
¾ teaspoon ground cloves

In bowl, mix together molasses, brown sugar, baking soda, ginger, and cinnamon until well blended. Cover and refrigerate for at least 15 minutes. Add about ¼ cup brewed coffee to mugs. Stir in 1 tablespoon of spice mixture until dissolved. Fill mug to within 1 inch of the top with coffee. Stir in half-and-half to taste. Garnish with whipped topping and ground cloves.

Choco-Cherry Coffee Mix

3 cups sugar
2 cups powdered sugar
1⅓ cups powdered nondairy
   creamer
1½ cups instant coffee granules

1 cup cocoa powder
1 packet unsweetened cherry
   drink mix
Miniature marshmallows
Red and green holiday sprinkles

In airtight container, combine first 6 ingredients. Store for up to 2 months. To prepare: Add ⅛ cup of drink mix to 1 cup hot milk. Garnish with miniature marshmallows and holiday sprinkles.

Honeyed Coffee

2 cups freshly brewed coffee
   (dark roast)
½ cup milk
¼ cup honey

¼ teaspoon ground cinnamon
Dash ground nutmeg
¼ teaspoon vanilla

In small saucepan, combine coffee, milk, honey, cinnamon, and nutmeg.
Cook and stir over medium heat until heated through (do not boil).
Remove from heat; stir in vanilla. Serve immediately.

Seasonal Teas

And they came with haste, and found Mary, and Joseph, and the babe lying in a manger. And when they had seen it, they made known abroad the saying which was told them concerning this child. And all they that heard it wondered at those things which were told them by the shepherds.

LUKE 2:16–18

Christmas Tea Mix

1 cup instant tea mix   ½ cup red cinnamon candies
2 cups powdered orange drink mix   ½ teaspoon ground cloves
3 cups sugar   1 packet lemonade mix

Mix ingredients and store in airtight container. To prepare: Add 1 heaping teaspoon to 1 cup hot water.

Holiday Breakfast Tea

3 cups water
3 regular tea bags
¼ cup orange marmalade

1 tablespoon lemon juice
1 tablespoon sugar
Lemon or orange slices

Bring water to boil in 2-quart saucepan. Add tea bags; cover and allow to steep for 3 to 5 minutes. Remove tea bags and add remaining ingredients; stir. Serve in mugs topped with lemon or orange slices.

Spiced Tea Mix

2 cups orange powdered drink mix
1 cup lemonade powdered
   drink mix
2 cups sugar

1 cup instant tea
1½ teaspoons cinnamon
¾ teaspoon ground cloves
½ cup red hot candies

Combine all ingredients in large bowl. To serve, pour 6 ounces boiling water over 4 teaspoons mix, stirring until well blended. Store mix in airtight container.

Russian Tea

1 cup sugar
1 cup water
25 whole cloves
1 quart weak tea

Juice of 1 lemon
Juice of 2 oranges
Pinch salt

Combine sugar, water, and cloves; simmer for 20 minutes.
Add to tea and fruit juices. Add pinch of salt.

Easy Sugar-Free Russian Tea Mix

4½ teaspoons sugar-free orange drink mix

3½ teaspoons sugar-free lemonade drink mix

Sugar substitute (equivalent to 16 teaspoons sugar)

1 teaspoon ground cinnamon

⅓ teaspoon ground cloves

Combine all ingredients and mix well. Store in airtight container. To prepare: Add ¼ teaspoon tea mix to ¾ cup hot water; stir well before serving.

Sunburst Spiced Tea

Zest from 2 oranges
Zest from 1 lemon
4 cardamom pods
3 to 4 whole cloves

4 teaspoons English Breakfast
Tea leaves
4 cups boiling water

Place orange and lemon zest, cardamom, and cloves in large bowl. With the end of a spoon handle, crush mixture until aromas are released. Add tea leaves and boiling water. Cover and steep for 5 to 6 minutes. Strain tea, discarding spice mixture. Serve immediately.

Grapefruit Tea

2 cups fresh red grapefruit juice
2 tablespoons honey
1 (3 inch) cinnamon stick

⅓ teaspoon whole allspice
½ cup water
Grapefruit zest

In medium saucepan, combine grapefruit juice, honey, cinnamon stick, allspice, and water. Bring to a boil then strain and discard spices. Serve in mugs with grapefruit zest garnish.

Orange Tea

7 cups water
1 (12 ounce) can frozen orange
   juice concentrate
½ cup sugar

2 tablespoons lemon juice
5 teaspoons instant tea mix
1 teaspoon whole cloves

In large saucepan, combine water, orange juice concentrate, sugar, lemon juice, and tea mix. Place cloves in tea ball or cheesecloth bag and add to saucepan. Simmer for 15 to 20 minutes. Remove cloves and serve hot.

Chocolate Chai

½ cup boiling water
1 bag black tea
3 tablespoons sugar
2 tablespoons cocoa powder

2 cups milk
1 teaspoon vanilla
½ teaspoon ground nutmeg
Whipped topping

In small saucepan, pour boiling water over tea bag. Cover and let stand for 3 to 5 minutes. Remove tea bag. Stir in sugar and cocoa. Cook and stir over medium heat just until mixture comes to a boil. Stir in milk, vanilla, and nutmeg; heat thoroughly (do not boil). Pour into mugs. Top with whipped topping.

Spiced Tea

4 bags orange pekoe tea
Juice of 3 oranges
Juice of 3 lemons
4 teaspoons ground cinnamon

1½ teaspoons ground cloves
2 cups sugar
16 cups (1 gallon) water

Combine all ingredients in large saucepan. Simmer for 20 minutes then
remove tea bags. Serve immediately.

Honey Citrus Green Tea

1 piece lemon zest, cut into
  thin strips
2 teaspoons boiling water
2 teaspoons green tea powder

¾ cup hot water
½ cup grapefruit juice
3½ tablespoons lemon juice
1 teaspoon honey

Put lemon zest in large mug. Cover with 2 teaspoons boiling water and let steep for about 4 minutes. Stir in green tea powder and hot water. Add grapefruit juice, lemon juice, and honey. Mix well and serve immediately.

Spearmint Tea

1 cup water	1 to 1½ teaspoons dried spearmint leaves

Bring water to boil in small saucepan. Remove from heat. Add spearmint leaves and let stand for 4 to 5 minutes. Strain tea into teacup.

Lemon Basil Tea

2 cups water	1½ tablespoons lemon zest
3 tablespoons thinly sliced fresh basil leaves	2 teaspoons English Breakfast Tea leaves

In small saucepan, bring water to boil. Remove from heat. Add fresh basil, lemon zest, and tea leaves; cover and steep for 5 minutes. Strain, discarding lemon zest and tea leaves. Serve immediately.

Apple Tea

1 cup water
4 whole allspice
2 black tea bags

1 cup unsweetened apple juice
1½ to 2 tablespoons honey

In small saucepan, bring water and allspice to boil; add tea bags. Remove from heat. Cover and steep for 3 to 4 minutes. Discard allspice and tea bags before stirring in apple juice and honey. Serve hot.

Spiced Apple Tea

2 cups unsweetened apple juice
5 whole cloves
1 cinnamon stick

3 cups water
5 tea bags
Additional cinnamon sticks

In small saucepan, combine apple juice, cloves, and 1 cinnamon stick. Bring to boil. Reduce heat and simmer uncovered for 15 minutes. Meanwhile, in large saucepan, bring water to boil. Remove from heat; add 5 tea bags. Cover and steep for 5 to 7 minutes; remove tea bags. Strain juice mixture, removing cloves and cinnamon. Stir into tea. Serve hot with cinnamon sticks.

1979 Cranberry Tea

1 pound cranberries or
  1 quart cranberry juice
3 quarts water, divided
1 cup hot cinnamon candies

½ cup lemon juice
2 cups sugar
10 whole cloves

Cook cranberries in 1 quart water until tender; strain and use juice.
Add remaining 2 quarts water and remaining ingredients; heat through
and serve. Use slow cooker to keep tea warm.

Vanilla Milk Tea

1 cup milk	4 teaspoons English Breakfast Tea
2 teaspoons vanilla	1 quart boiling water

Simmer milk and vanilla in small saucepan, stirring often. Remove from heat and allow to stand until milk is cool. Ready teapot and teacups with hot water; drain and dry. Place tea in teapot and add boiling water. Cover with tea towel and steep for 5 minutes. Pour ½ cup of cold milk into teacups. Strain tea into hot cups and serve.

Ginger Tea

1 cup water
2 teaspoons honey
1 teaspoon ground ginger

3 tea bags
¾ cup milk

Bring water to boil in small saucepan. Add honey and ginger.
Reduce heat; cover and simmer for 8 to 10 minutes. Remove from heat;
add tea bags. Cover and steep for 5 to 7 minutes. Discard tea bags.
Stir in milk and heat through (do not boil) before serving.

Peach Tea Mix

1 cup instant tea mix   2 cups sugar
1 (3 ounce) box peach gelatin

Combine all ingredients and mix well. Store in airtight container.
To prepare: Combine 2 teaspoons of tea mix with 1 cup hot water.
Serve immediately.

Spicy Chocolate Tea

1 cup fat free milk
1 cup water
2 regular tea bags
1 tablespoon sugar

1 teaspoon chocolate syrup
⅛ teaspoon ground cinnamon
⅛ teaspoon ground ginger
⅛ teaspoon ground nutmeg

Bring milk and water to boil in 2-quart saucepan. Remove from heat and add tea bags. Cover and steep for 5 minutes. Remove tea bags; stir in remaining ingredients. Serve immediately.

Mochas, Lattes & Other Holiday Beverages

*For unto us a child is born, unto us a son is given. . .
and his name shall be called Wonderful.*

Isaiah 9:6

Fireside Mocha Mix

2 cups powdered nondairy creamer   1½ cups sugar
1½ cups instant coffee granules   1 teaspoon ground cinnamon
1½ cups instant hot chocolate mix   ¼ teaspoon ground nutmeg

In large bowl, combine all ingredients. Store mixture in airtight container.
To prepare: Stir 2 heaping tablespoons of mix into 1 cup boiling water.

Hot Christmas Punch

1½ quarts water
2 cups sugar
Juice of 3 oranges
Juice of 1 lemon

4 ounces red cinnamon candies
1 (20 ounce) can pineapple juice
2 quarts cranberry juice

In large saucepan, boil water, sugar, orange juice, lemon juice, and cinnamon candies. Stir and boil until candies are dissolved. Add in pineapple juice and cranberry juice and cook over medium heat, stirring until punch is thoroughly heated. Serve hot.

Steaming Hot Holiday Punch

3 cups apple juice
3 cups orange juice
6 cups cranberry juice cocktail
¾ cup maple syrup
2 teaspoons powdered sugar

½ teaspoon ground cinnamon
¾ teaspoon ground cloves
¾ teaspoon ground nutmeg
Cinnamon sticks (optional)

Combine all ingredients in large saucepan, except for cinnamon sticks. Bring to boil. Reduce to simmer for a few minutes. Keep warm in slow cooker if desired. Cinnamon sticks may be used as stirrers if desired.

Chocolate Mint Latte

¾ ounce chocolate mint syrup   Steamed milk
1 to 2 shots espresso

Pour flavored syrup into mug. Add espresso—1 to 2 shots, depending on
your taste. Stir. Top with foamy, steamed milk. Serve.

Black Forest Mocha

⅔ cup hot brewed coffee   1 tablespoon maraschino
2 tablespoons chocolate syrup   cherry juice
2 tablespoons light cream   Whipped topping

In large mug, stir together coffee, chocolate syrup, cream, and cherry juice.
Garnish with whipped topping. Serve immediately.

Merry Christmas Drink Mix

2½ cups nonfat dry milk powder
2½ cups pastel miniature
  marshmallows
1 cup strawberry drink mix

½ cup powdered sugar
⅓ cup buttermilk blend powder
⅓ cup powdered nondairy creamer

In large mixing bowl, combine all ingredients. Store in airtight container for up to 6 months. To prepare: Mix ⅓ cup drink mix with ¾ cup boiling water. Stir well.

Christmas Morning Mocha

6 cups freshly brewed coffee
¾ cup half-and-half
5 tablespoons chocolate syrup

7 teaspoons sugar
6 cinnamon sticks
Whipped topping

In large saucepan, combine coffee, half-and-half, chocolate syrup, and sugar. Cook and stir over medium heat until mixture is heated through (do not boil). Serve in mugs and garnish with cinnamon sticks and whipped topping.

Mint Mocha

1 cup water
⅓ cup sugar
6 chocolate mint candies
¾ cup half-and-half

¾ cup milk
2 cups freshly brewed coffee
Whipped topping
Miniature chocolate chips

In large saucepan, combine water, sugar, and candies. Cook and stir until sugar is dissolved and candies are melted. Add half-and-half and milk; stir and heat through. Pour in coffee. Serve in mugs with whipped topping and miniature chocolate chips.

Mexi-Mocha

1 cup packed brown sugar
4 ounces semisweet chocolate
  chips
2 (3 inch) orange peel strips
½ teaspoon ground cinnamon

¼ teaspoon ground allspice
3 cups freshly brewed strong coffee
½ cup half-and-half, warmed
Whipped topping

Place first 6 ingredients in blender; cover and process until chocolate
is melted. Transfer to small saucepan and heat through. Return mixture
to blender; add warmed half-and-half. Cover and process until frothy.
Strain and discard any remaining solids before serving.
Garnish with whipped topping.

Very Berry Mocha

1 (1 ounce) packet instant hot
   chocolate mix
1 tablespoon instant coffee
   granules

1 cup boiling water
2 tablespoons strawberry syrup
Whipped topping

Combine hot chocolate mix and instant coffee in large mug. Carefully pour boiling water into mug; stir until dissolved. Stir in fruit syrup. Garnish with whipped topping and serve immediately.

Crème Brulée Latte

2 tablespoons caramel topping, divided
1 ounce vanilla syrup

2 ounces espresso or strong coffee
8 ounces steamed milk

Lace sides of mug with 1 tablespoon caramel topping. Place vanilla syrup at bottom of mug and top with espresso or coffee. Heat milk by steaming it using an espresso machine or by slowly heating it over medium heat and then whipping it until desired amount of froth is created. Fill cup with steamed milk and top with remaining caramel.

Caramel Brown Sugar Latte

1 tablespoon brown sugar   1 tablespoon caramel syrup
¼ cup half-and-half   Whipped topping
¾ cup freshly brewed coffee

Whisk brown sugar into half-and-half until completely dissolved.
Pour coffee into mug and stir in caramel syrup. Pour half-and-half and
sugar mix into coffee. Serve immediately with whipped topping if desired.

Eggnog Latte

⅓ cup milk   1½ ounces freshly brewed espresso
⅔ cup eggnog   Pinch ground nutmeg

Heat milk and eggnog by slowly heating mixture over medium
heat and then whipping until desired amount of froth is created.
Add freshly brewed espresso to mug. Top off with milk/eggnog
mixture, using spoon to hold back the foam. Spoon foam over
top and sprinkle with ground nutmeg if desired.

Hot Vanilla

4 cups milk
4 teaspoons honey

½ teaspoon vanilla
Ground cinnamon

In saucepan, heat milk until very hot (do not boil). Remove from heat and stir in honey and vanilla. Divide between 4 mugs and sprinkle with cinnamon.

Hot Strawberry Malt

¾ cup milk
1 tablespoon instant malted
  milk powder

2 cups strawberry ice cream, divided

In small saucepan, stir together milk and malted milk powder. Add 1 cup of strawberry ice cream. Cook and stir over medium-low heat about 5 to 7 minutes or until ice cream is melted and mixture is hot. Divide remaining ice cream between 2 mugs and top off with hot milk mixture. Serve immediately.

Chai Latte

1 cup milk
1 cup water
1 strip orange peel
3 whole cloves
1 (2 inch) cinnamon stick

3 whole black peppercorns
1 pinch ground nutmeg
4 teaspoons sugar
2 teaspoons black tea leaves

Combine milk and water in saucepan over medium-high heat. Once mixture has warmed, add orange peel, cloves, cinnamon stick, peppercorns, nutmeg, sugar, and tea leaves. Bring to boil then reduce heat and simmer until color deepens. Strain out spices and pour into cups. Serve.

Spicy Orange-Apple Punch

1½ quarts orange juice
1 quart apple juice
⅓ cup light corn syrup

24 whole cloves
6 cinnamon sticks
12 thin lemon slices

Combine orange and apple juices, corn syrup, cloves, and cinnamon sticks in large saucepan. Gradually bring to boil. Reduce heat and simmer at least 5 to 10 minutes to blend flavors. Strain out cloves and cinnamon. Serve hot with a lemon slice.

Hot Apple Cider

2 quarts apple cider   8 whole allspice
8 whole cloves   1 stick cinnamon

Combine ingredients in large saucepan. Bring to boil. Reduce heat and
simmer uncovered for 10 to 20 minutes. Remove spices before serving.

Apricot Apple Cider

8 cups unsweetened apple juice
1 (12 ounce) can ginger ale
½ cup dried apricots
½ cup dried cranberries

3 cinnamon sticks
1 tablespoon whole allspice
1 tablespoon whole cloves

In slow cooker, combine apple juice and ginger ale. Place apricots, cranberries, cinnamon sticks, allspice, and cloves on double thickness of cheesecloth, bringing up corners of cloth and tying with string to form a bag. Place in apple juice mixture. Cover and cook on high for 4 hours or until heated through. Discard spice bag before serving.

Hot and Spicy Cherry Cider

1 gallon apple cider   2 (3 ounce) packages cherry gelatin
3 cinnamon sticks

Place cider in 6-quart slow cooker; add cinnamon sticks. Cover and cook
on high for 2 to 3 hours. Stir in gelatin; cook an additional hour.
Discard cinnamon sticks before serving.

Strawberry Cider

8 cups apple cider   1 (3 inch) cinnamon stick
¾ teaspoon whole cloves   1 pound frozen strawberries

Bring all ingredients to boil. Reduce to low heat and simmer
for 10 to 12 minutes. Strain to remove pulp. Serve hot.

Cinnamon-Orange Cider

4 cups apple juice
2 cups orange juice
3 tablespoons cinnamon candies

1½ teaspoons whole allspice
4½ teaspoons honey

In large saucepan, combine juices and candies. Place allspice on double thickness of cheesecloth, bringing up corners of cloth and tying with string to form bag. Add to pan. Bring liquid to boil. Reduce heat; cover and simmer for 5 minutes. Discard spice bag then stir in honey. Serve immediately or transfer to slow cooker to keep warm.

Buttery Orange Cider

6 cups apple juice
½ medium unpeeled orange,
 sliced
6 whole allspice
6 whole cloves

2 cinnamon sticks
1 (3 inch) orange peel strip
½ cup packed brown sugar
¼ cup butter, softened
½ teaspoon ground cinnamon

In large saucepan, combine apple juice and orange slices. Place allspice, cloves, cinnamon sticks, and orange peel on double thickness of cheesecloth, bringing up corners of cloth and tying with kitchen string to form bag. Add to juice. Bring to boil over medium heat. Reduce heat and simmer uncovered for 15 minutes. In small bowl, combine brown sugar, butter, and cinnamon. Discard spice bag before serving. Serve in mugs topped with cinnamon-sugar mixture.

Spiced Apricot Cider

2 (12 ounce) cans apricot nectar
2 cups water
¼ cup lemon juice

¼ cup sugar
2 whole cloves
2 (3 inch) cinnamon sticks

Combine all ingredients in slow cooker and mix well. Cook covered
for 2 hours. Remove cloves and cinnamon sticks. Serve hot.

Spiced Apple-Grape Juice

4 cups white grape juice
3 cups unsweetened apple juice
1 cup water

2 cinnamon sticks
10 whole cloves
8 whole allspice

In large saucepan, combine grape juice, apple juice, and water. Place cinnamon, cloves, and allspice on double thickness of cheesecloth, bringing up corners of cloth and tying with string to form bag. Add to juice mixture and bring to boil. Reduce heat and simmer uncovered for 1 hour or until flavors are blended. Discard spice bag before serving.

Caramel Latte

1 tablespoon brown sugar
¼ cup half-and-half
¾ cup freshly brewed coffee

1 tablespoon caramel ice-cream
topping

Stir brown sugar into half-and-half until dissolved. Whip with small whisk. Pour coffee into mug and stir in caramel sauce until dissolved. Pour half-and-half/brown sugar mixture into coffee and serve.

S'More Latte

2 cups freshly brewed coffee
¾ cup half-and-half
¼ cup chocolate syrup
⅛ teaspoon ground cinnamon

Miniature marshmallows
2 chocolate-covered graham cracker
   cookies, crushed

Combine first 4 ingredients in 2-quart saucepan. Cook over medium heat, stirring constantly until mixture begins to boil. Remove from heat. Pour into mugs and top with miniature marshmallows and crushed cookies.

Triple Berry Latte

½ ounce blueberry syrup
½ ounce strawberry syrup
½ ounce raspberry syrup

2 shots espresso
Steamed milk

Pour syrup into mug. Add espresso and swirl to mix. Top with steamed milk. Serve.

Blanco Latte

½ cup milk
2 tablespoons hazelnut syrup
1 scoop hazelnut ice cream

Whipped topping
Ground nutmeg

In small pan, steam milk until it foams. Pour syrup into mug. Add ice cream. Gently pour in steamed milk and spoon foam on top. (Do not stir.) Serve with whipped topping sprinkled with ground nutmeg.

Winter White Chocolate Latte

1½ cups whole milk
1 tablespoon heavy cream
⅛ teaspoon vanilla
1 tablespoon sugar

½ cup freshly brewed espresso
⅓ cup miniature white
    chocolate chips

Combine milk and cream in medium saucepan; stir over high heat until frothy. Remove from heat and stir in vanilla and sugar. Whisk together espresso and white chocolate chips in mug until smooth. Pour into mug and top with hot milk mixture. Stir to blend. Serve immediately.

Wassail

1 gallon apple cider
2 cups orange juice
1 (6 ounce) can frozen lemonade
 concentrate

2 teaspoons ground cinnamon
1 teaspoon ground nutmeg
1 teaspoon ground cloves
1 orange, cut into slices

Mix all ingredients in large saucepan and slowly bring to boil. Simmer for
10 minutes. Float orange slices in hot wassail before serving.

Winter White Wassail

1 (64 ounce) bottle white
    cranberry juice
3 (3 inch) cinnamon sticks
¼ teaspoon ground ginger

6 teaspoons butter, softened
6 teaspoons brown sugar
Additional cinnamon sticks

Combine juice, cinnamon sticks, and ginger in large saucepan. Bring to boil then reduce heat and simmer for 10 to 12 minutes. Put 1 teaspoon each of butter and brown sugar in 6 large mugs; top off with drink mixture. Stir gently. Serve with a cinnamon stick garnish.

Gingerbread Wassail

1 large orange with peel,
   cut into 8 pieces
1 large lemon with peel,
   cut into 8 pieces
2 cinnamon sticks, broken
   into small pieces

¼ teaspoon ground allspice
¼ teaspoon ginger
32 ounces all-natural apple juice

Place all ingredients in slow cooker. Heat on low until heated through—
about 1½ hours. Serve warm.

Cozy Raspberry Lemon Drink Mix

1½ cups sweetened lemonade mix   1 cup instant tea mix
1 (1.3 ounce) carton raspberry
    drink mix

In large bowl, combine all ingredients. Mix well. Store in airtight
container for up to 3 months. To prepare: Dissolve 1 teaspoon of
drink mix with 1 cup boiling water.

Breakfast Wassail

1 (64 ounce) can cranberry juice   1 (12 ounce) can frozen lemonade
1 (32 ounce) can apple juice   concentrate, undiluted
1 (12 ounce) can frozen pineapple   4 cinnamon sticks
    juice concentrate, undiluted

In large saucepan, combine juices and cinnamon sticks. Bring to boil.
Reduce heat; cover and simmer for approximately 1 hour. Serve hot.

English Wassail

3 oranges
Whole cloves
3 quarts apple cider
2 (3 inch) cinnamon sticks
½ teaspoon ground nutmeg

½ cup honey
⅓ cup lemon juice
2 teaspoons lemon zest
5 cups pineapple juice

Stud oranges with cloves about ½ inch apart. Place in baking pan with a little water. Bake slowly for 30 minutes. Heat cider and cinnamon sticks in large saucepan. Bring to boil. Simmer uncovered for 5 minutes. Add remaining ingredients and simmer uncovered for 5 additional minutes. Pour into punchbowl; float spiced oranges on top. Use cinnamon sticks for stirring. If desired, keep wassail hot in slow cooker.

Gingerbread Latte

2 ounces espresso
2 tablespoons gingerbread
   flavored syrup
½ cup steamed milk

⅛ cup whipped cream
1 pinch ground cinnamon
1 pinch ground nutmeg
½ teaspoon vanilla powder

In mug, combine espresso with syrup. Pour in steamed milk.
Top with whipped cream then sprinkle with cinnamon,
nutmeg, and vanilla powder. Serve.

Hot Cranberry Cider

1 quart apple cider
1 (32 ounce) bottle cranberry juice
½ cup lemon juice
½ cup firmly packed light
   brown sugar

8 whole cloves
2 cinnamon sticks

Combine ingredients in large saucepan. Bring to boil. Reduce heat and
simmer uncovered for 10 minutes. Remove spices before serving.

Hot Caramel Apple Drink

4 cups apple cider   1½ cups caramel sauce

Bring apple cider to simmer in medium pan over medium heat.
Add caramel sauce and stir until melted. Remove from heat and serve
immediately.

Lemon Cider

1 gallon apple juice   1 lemon, thinly sliced
1 (12 ounce) can frozen lemonade
   concentrate, thawed

In slow cooker, combine apple juice and lemonade concentrate. Set cooker
on low until heated through. Float lemon slices on top before serving.

Pomegranate Punch

4 cups pomegranate juice
3½ to 4 cups unsweetened
   apple juice
2 cups freshly brewed tea

½ cup sugar
⅓ cup lemon juice
3 cinnamon sticks
10 whole cloves

In 4-quart slow cooker, combine first 5 ingredients. Place and secure cinnamon sticks and cloves in cheesecloth. Add to slow cooker. Cover and cook on low for 4 hours or until heated through. Discard spice bag. Serve warm.

Mulled Pomegranate-Apple Cider

1 (64 ounce) bottle cran–apple juice
2 cups unsweetened apple juice
1 cup pomegranate juice
½ cup honey
½ cup orange juice
3 cinnamon sticks
8 whole cloves
2 tablespoons orange zest

In 5-quart slow cooker, combine first 5 ingredients. Place cinnamon sticks, cloves, and orange zest on double thickness of cheesecloth, bringing up corners of cloth and tying with string to form bag. Add to juice mixture. Cover and cook on low for 1½ hours. Discard spice bag before serving.

Pumpkin Spice Latte

1 shot (1 to 1.5 ounce) brewed
espresso
2 tablespoons canned pumpkin
puree

1 teaspoon vanilla
2 tablespoons sugar
¼ teaspoon pumpkin pie spice
1 cup milk

While preparing espresso, whisk together pumpkin, vanilla, sugar,
pumpkin pie spice, and milk in small saucepan over medium heat.
Stir constantly until hot and frothy (do not boil). Pour espresso
into mug and top off with pumpkin mixture.

Sweet Dreams

1 cup milk
1¼ teaspoon honey

2 drops vanilla
Pinch ground cinnamon

Pour milk into microwave-safe mug; warm in microwave on high until milk is very hot—approximately 2½ to 3 minutes. Stir in honey and vanilla. Sprinkle with ground cinnamon before serving.

Amaretto Fudge Cappuccino

1 cup boiling water
1 tablespoon instant coffee
  granules

2 tablespoons amaretto-flavored
  creamer
1 tablespoon chocolate syrup

Combine water and coffee in mug; stir until coffee is dissolved.
Stir in creamer and chocolate syrup. Serve immediately.

Raspberry Truffle Latte

6 ounces freshly brewed coffee
2 tablespoons chocolate syrup
2 tablespoons raspberry syrup
½ cup (4 ounces) chocolate
  ice cream

Whipped topping
Grated chocolate
Fresh raspberries

Mix coffee and flavored syrups in mug. Spoon ice cream into coffee
mixture. Add whipped topping, grated chocolate, and fresh raspberries as
desired. Serve immediately.

Hot Cappuccino Mix

1 cup instant hot chocolate mix
½ cup instant coffee granules
½ cup powdered nondairy
  creamer
½ cup powdered skim milk

1¼ teaspoons ground cinnamon
¼ teaspoon ground nutmeg
Boiling water
Grated chocolate (optional)

Mix dry ingredients well and store in airtight container. To prepare:
Use ¼ cup mixture for each 2 cups boiling water. Blend desired amount
until foamy; pour into mugs. Sprinkle with grated chocolate if desired.

Honey-Nut Latte

1 ounce hazelnut syrup
1 ounce honey
1 to 2 ounces espresso
Steamed milk

Whipped topping
Honey to taste
Nuts, finely chopped

In large mug, mix hazelnut syrup and honey with hot espresso; stir until honey dissolves. Fill mug with steamed milk. Garnish with whipped topping, honey, and nuts.

Holiday Eggnog

2 cups sugar
8 eggs
2 cups whole milk
½ tablespoon ground nutmeg

½ tablespoon ground cinnamon
½ teaspoon ground cloves
2 cups whipped topping

Whip sugar, eggs, and milk together on high speed for approximately 13 to 15 minutes. Place over low heat, stirring constantly until heated through. Cool; add spices and whipped topping. Beat until foamy. Serve immediately.

Honey and Spice Latte

½ cup ground coffee
1½ cups cold water
1⅓ cups milk
2 tablespoons honey
2 tablespoons molasses
4 teaspoons sugar

¼ teaspoon ground ginger
⅓ teaspoon ground cinnamon
⅛ teaspoon ground nutmeg
⅛ teaspoon ground cloves
Whipped topping

Place ground coffee in filter of coffeemaker. Add water and brew according to manufacturer's instructions. In small saucepan, combine remaining ingredients except whipped topping. Cook and stir over medium heat until hot (do not boil). Remove from heat then transfer to blender; cover and process until foamy. Add to freshly brewed coffee. Pour into mugs and serve with whipped topping.

Grandma's Hot Milk

1 cup milk

1 teaspoon vanilla

2½ tablespoons sugar

¼ teaspoon ground nutmeg

In mug, stir together milk, vanilla, and sugar. Heat in microwave on high for 1 to 2 minutes. Stir in nutmeg. Serve.

Hot Almond and Cream Drink

1 cup butter
1 cup sugar
1 cup packed brown sugar

2 cups vanilla ice cream, softened
2 teaspoons almond extract
Ground nutmeg

Over low heat, cook and stir butter and sugars for 10 minutes or until butter is melted. Pour into large bowl; add ice cream and almond extract. Beat on medium speed until smooth, scraping bowl often. To prepare: Spoon ¼ cup mix into mug; add ¾ cup boiling water. Stir well. Sprinkle with ground nutmeg before serving.

Hot Cranberry Beverage

3 quarts water
3 cups fresh cranberries
3 lemons, sliced
3 oranges, sliced

12 whole cloves
3 (2 inch) cinnamon sticks
2 cups honey
1 teaspoon ground nutmeg

In dutch oven, mix water, cranberries, lemons, and oranges. Bring to boil. Allow to cook until cranberry skins break open. Strain mixture. Place cloves and cinnamon sticks in spice bag. Add to dutch oven. Add honey and nutmeg to dutch oven. Cook over medium heat for 10 minutes, stirring occasionally. Remove spice bag and serve immediately.

Grape Cider

4½ pounds Concord grapes
8 cups water, divided
1½ cups sugar

8 whole cloves
4 cinnamon sticks
Dash ground nutmeg

In large saucepan, combine grapes and 2 cups water; bring to boil, stirring constantly. Press through strainer, reserving juice only. Pour juice through cheesecloth into 5-quart slow cooker. Add sugar, cloves, cinnamon sticks, nutmeg, and remaining water. Cover and cook on low for approximately 3 hours. Before serving, discard cloves and cinnamon sticks.

Cherry Chocolate Cappuccino

3 cups sugar
2 cups powdered sugar
1⅓ cups powdered nondairy
    creamer

1⅓ cups instant coffee granules
1 cup cocoa powder
1 packet unsweetened cherry
    drink mix

In large, airtight container, combine all ingredients. Store for up to 2 months. To prepare: For each serving, place 2 tablespoons cappuccino mix in bottom of mug. Stir in 1 cup hot milk until combined. Top with miniature marshmallows if desired.

Warm Tea Punch

1½ cups water
6 orange herbal tea bags
8 to 10 whole cloves
2 cinnamon sticks

2 cups cranberry juice
1½ cups white grape juice
½ cup packed brown sugar
Orange slices

Bring water to boil in medium saucepan. Remove from heat; add tea bags, cloves, and cinnamon sticks. Cover and steep for 5 to 7 minutes. Remove tea bags. Stir in cranberry and white grape juices and brown sugar; heat through. Remove spices. Garnish with orange slices if desired.

Toasty Sugar-Free Cappuccino Shake

1 cup milk
1½ teaspoons instant coffee
   granules
Sugar substitute (equivalent to
   4 teaspoons sugar)

2 drops brandy extract
Dash ground cinnamon

Combine milk, coffee granules, sweetener, and brandy extract in blender. Process until coffee is dissolved. Pour into mug and heat in microwave before serving. Garnish with a dash of cinnamon.

Instant Latte

1 cup nonfat dry milk powder   ⅓ cup sugar
½ cup powdered nondairy creamer   ¼ cup instant vanilla pudding mix
⅓ cup instant coffee granules

Combine all ingredients. Place in blender; cover and process until mixture is a fine powder. Store in airtight container for up to 6 months. To prepare: Dissolve ¼ cup latte mix in hot water; stir.

Cold &
Christmassy
Beverages

Once on royal David's city
Stood a lowly cattle shed,
Where a mother laid her baby
In a manger for his bed:
Mary was that mother mild,
Jesus Christ her little child.

CECIL FRANCES ALEXANDER

Easy Peppermint Mocha Frappuccino

1 cup whole milk
1 scoop of chocolate powdered
   drink mix
2 tablespoons instant coffee
   granules

2 tablespoons chocolate syrup
1 ounce peppermint syrup
1 cup crushed ice

Place all ingredients in blender. Mix thoroughly. Pour into tall glass and serve immediately.

Mocha Coconut Frappuccino

½ cup shredded coconut, divided
¾ cup dark roast coffee, chilled
1 cup milk
⅓ cup chocolate syrup

3 tablespoons sugar
2 cups crushed ice
½ cup whipped topping
Chocolate syrup

Spread shredded coconut on baking sheet and toast at 300 degrees for 25 minutes, stirring every 10 minutes for even browning. Remove from oven and cool. Prepare coffee; chill. Combine cold coffee, milk, ⅓ cup of toasted coconut, ⅓ cup chocolate syrup, and sugar in blender. Blend for 25 seconds until sugar is dissolved. Add ice and blend until smooth. Pour drinks into tall glasses. Garnish with whipped topping, a drizzle of chocolate syrup, and a pinch of toasted coconut. Serve immediately.

Pumpkin Frappuccino

3 teaspoons sugar
1 tablespoon vanilla syrup
½ cup freshly brewed espresso
¾ cup milk

1 cup crushed ice
3 tablespoons canned pumpkin
Dash pumpkin pie spice

Dissolve sugar and syrup in hot espresso. Add milk and refrigerate until cold. Add cooled coffee mixture, ice, pumpkin, and pumpkin pie spice in blender and blend on high until smooth. Pour into tall glass and serve immediately.

White Christmas Drink

2 cups whole milk   1 teaspoon vanilla
¾ cup sugar   1 full tray ice cubes

Add all ingredients to blender and blend on high until smooth.
Pour into tall glasses and serve immediately.

Peppermint Eggnog Punch

1 quart peppermint-flavored
   ice cream, divided
1 quart prepared eggnog

4 (12 ounce) cans ginger ale, chilled
Miniature candy canes

Place 2 scoops of ice cream (to be used for garnish) in small bowl and place back in freezer. Place remaining ice cream in large mixing bowl and stir until softened. Gradually stir in eggnog. Transfer mixture to punch bowl and add ginger ale. Decorate edges of punchbowl with miniature candy canes. Remove reserved ice cream from freezer and float on top of punch. Serve immediately.

Hot Chocolate Milkshake

2 cups whole milk
4 tablespoons instant hot
   chocolate mix

2 scoops of chocolate ice cream
Whipped topping
Miniature chocolate chips

Blend milk and drink mix in blender on medium speed for 3 minutes.
Gradually add 2 scoops of chocolate ice cream and blend until smooth.
Pour into tall glass and top with whipped topping
and miniature chocolate chips.

Frozen Gingerbread Cappuccino

1 scoop vanilla ice cream
1 ounce gingerbread flavored
  syrup
1 ounce espresso

1½ cups crushed ice
Gingerbread cookie, crushed

Add first 4 ingredients to blender and mix on high until smooth.
Pour into tall glass and top with crushed gingerbread cookie pieces.
Serve immediately.

Snowman Milkshake

2 cups vanilla ice cream
2 ounces milk
1 ounce chocolate syrup

1 ounce peppermint syrup
Whipped topping
Miniature chocolate chips

Combine first 4 ingredients in blender. Blend on high until smooth.
Pour into tall glass and serve topped with whipped topping and
miniature chocolate chips.

Candy Cane Milkshake

2 candy canes, crushed
¾ cup whole milk
2 scoops vanilla ice cream

Whipped topping
Red and green holiday sprinkles

Place first 3 ingredients in blender and blend until smooth. Pour into tall glass and top with whipped topping and sprinkles. Serve immediately.

North Pole Smoothie

1 (10 ounce) package frozen
    strawberries in syrup, partially
    thawed and undrained
¼ cup water

2 cups vanilla frozen yogurt
2 tablespoons vanilla yogurt
1 strawberry-flavored candy cane,
    crushed

Place strawberries and water in blender; cover and blend on medium until smooth. Pour strawberry mixture into bowl and set aside. After cleaning blender, add frozen yogurt and vanilla yogurt in blender; cover and blend on medium until smooth. Pour strawberry and yogurt mixture into tall glasses at the same time. Serve topped with crushed strawberry candy cane pieces.

Pumpkin Pie Milkshake

⅓ cup canned pumpkin

12 cups whole milk

¼ teaspoon vanilla

½ teaspoon ground cinnamon

⅛ teaspoon pumpkin pie spice

2 tablespoons brown sugar

2 cups vanilla ice cream

Graham crackers, crushed

Blend all ingredients except for graham crackers in blender until smooth.
Pour into tall glass and serve topped with graham cracker pieces.

Eggnog Shake

1 cup prepared eggnog
¼ teaspoon vanilla

1½ scoops vanilla ice cream
Ground nutmeg

In blender combine first 3 ingredients and mix until smooth. Pour into tall glass and sprinkle with nutmeg. Serve immediately.

Coffee Milkshake

2 scoops vanilla ice cream
½ cup milk

1 teaspoon instant coffee granules
Dash cinnamon

Blend ice cream, milk, coffee, and cinnamon in blender until smooth.
Pour into tall glass and serve immediately.

Notes

Notes

Notes

Notes

Notes

Notes

Notes

Notes

Recipe Index

Hot Cocoa Delights

Christmassy Coffee Drinks

Seasonal Teas

Mochas, Lattes & Other Holiday Beverages

Cold & Christmassy Beverages